Discovering and Walking in Purpose

Book Five of the Duncan-Williams Youth Series

Archbishop Nicholas Duncan-Williams

A GOSHEN PUBLISHERS PAPERBACK   VIRGINIA

Discovering and Walking in Purpose
Book Five

ISBN: 978-1-7342639-1-6

Published in 2019
by:

GOSHEN PUBLISHERS LLC
P.O. Box 1562
Stephens City, Virginia, USA
www.GoshenPublishers.com

Our books may be purchased in bulk for promotional, educational, or business use. Please email Agents@GoshenPublishers.com.

First Edition 2019

Cover designed by Goshen Publishers LLC

The Duncan-Williams Youth Series seeks, among several others, to bless you in the following ways:

1. Help you totally yield your life and your future to God, trusting and depending wholly on Him;

2. Equip and challenge you to build and maintain a vibrant intimate relationship with God so you can navigate the journey of life more decisively;

3. Help you become a man or woman of prayer, drawing power from your fellowship with God to deal with situations in your life;

4. Get you to pay closer attention to the value of the family of God on earth, so

you can stay with the brethren and not become an easy target of the enemy;

5. Help you identify sin in its forms and resolve to confront sin with the principles and power of God;

6. Dare you to be different in your generation that is heavily influenced by immorality and godlessness, and thereby walk in integrity, honoring God in your life always;

7. Assist you to discover and develop your God-given talents and spiritual gifts by which you can offer acceptable service in the house of God;

8. Help you develop Christian character as the foundation for a future life of leadership and purpose;

9. Challenge you to share your faith in Christ as per the gospel, and God's power unto salvation without fear, and become a good evangelist for God;

10. Help you know how to draw strength from the Holy Spirit, stand in the position of authority, and walk in victory in all the issues confronting you as a growing person; and

11. Help you understand and develop healthful habits in relating with the opposite sex, and thereby prepare for a meaningful marriage and family life.

DISCOVERING AND WALKING IN PURPOSE

Book Five

Other publications in this series:

All by Archbishop Nicholas Duncan-Williams

This book belongs to

_____

[Name]

CONTENTS

INTRODUCTION

What would you do if after completing your university education you were still at a loss as to what to do with your life? In other words, is it possible that someone can go as far as completing tertiary education and still not know exactly what one is doing with one's life?

There are several examples of people like that walking on earth. Wait a minute! Do not blame them. Some of them may be victims of life's circumstances. Some probably made the wrong choices, but there are many people who have not made good choices in life.

In this book of my *Youth Classic Series*, I want to address the topic that will help you avoid going through life with no purpose in mind. I don't want you to follow the crowd or do what you see others do.

The understanding I want you to have as you read this book is that you are not on earth by chance. God has said in many places in Scriptures that He has plans for each of us. In His desire to partner with people to carry out His purposes, God calls people and equips them to be able to represent Him on earth. God works with such people on earth as His partners to carry out His purpose for humanity.

We identify such people as icons who have influenced situations in this life. Sometimes we call them leaders of their generation. Some of them become aware of being partners with God; and it shows in their positive attitudes and especially how they relate with the rest of humanity with dignity.

Others are not even conscious that it is God who has privileged them to work alongside with Him. They refuse to acknowledge God in anything and take all the glory unto themselves.

The problem with most people is that they look elsewhere instead of looking to God and what He is saying concerning them. Meaningful life starts when one discovers his purpose for life. Without that, you will walk through the routines of this life and get yourself frustrated with doing things, and changing from one thing to the other in a meaningless way.

You have to start seeing yourself as someone God wants to partner with to carry out His purposes on earth. That is the mindset you need as you read along.

I pray for you that having read the earlier books in this series up to this point, you will be in position to start living a more meaningful life than you have prior to this time.

Enjoy reading and be blessed by every sentence you encounter in this book.

1.

Discovering my Passion/Purpose

I am sure at some point you have been asked the question about what you want to become when you grow up. Go back down memory lane and recall the answers you gave.

1. _____

2. _____

3. _____

4. _____

5. _____

During those years when people tend to respond under the influence of fantasy, you find people mentioning some of the professions they are exposed to.

A growing child's world is often influenced by the adults surrounding him or her. So, whatever they hear the parents and the adult world commonly talk about is what they say as their choice. Sometimes they are influenced also by the value their parents put on the careers they talk about.

If your parents talk about the virtues of being a doctor, you find growing persons thinking they want to become a doctor. The same goes with vocations like engineering, architecture, pilot, entrepreneur, etc.

Those are the common ones that most adults want their children to be thinking about. They are influenced mostly by the prestige society associates with those professions and to a large extent the remuneration that is usually associated with those professions and careers.

You commonly find people saying, for example, that teachers and nurses are not paid well. When growing people hear those statements, expect them to take those professions out of their options. Guess what? A lot of people find themselves in those professions and they do very well in them, too. This means that there is something basically wrong with the parameters we use to identify what we want to become in the future or, in other words, how we want to spend or lives on earth.

The principle that can guide and help people make good choices for their future is that they should be exposed to as many situations as possible. Instead of parents talking about only one profession with their children, they should talk about all.

I am sure that if your parents exposed you to as many possible careers as possible you would have been placed in a good position to make a good choice for yourself.

It is a common experience, for example, to see students enrolled in a program at the university because that is what their parents insisted they do.

One way to discover your passion is to take a visit to several places that engage services for people. These might include a hospital, bank, building construction site, law court, school, church, natural forest service, music and drama production, farm plantation, food processing factory, etc.

Identifying your Passion

Let me make a correction here. Your passion is not the career name. Your passion is not to become an architect. The passion is the underlying factor inside your heart that pushes you to choose a particular career by which that passion will be executed. Your passion is what you feel is your contribution in the lives of people to make them better than before you met them.

Let me take you back down memory lane. For all the places you visited when you were growing up; whether by your parents or teachers or a club or association you belonged to, pause and reflect over the following questions:

1. Identify the places that made a deeper impact on you. What were the things in particular that touched your heart in all these places?

_____

_____

_____

2. Of the places you visited, which of them was on your mind several days after the visit? In other words, if you had the chance again, which of them would you like to visit?

_____

_____

_____

3. What did you see in particular that made you angry and you felt deeply obligated to respond by doing something to change and, possibly, totally eliminate?

_____

_____

_____

4. Did you tell yourself and perhaps utter a simple statement that you did not see as a prayer? Maybe you just said that if God grants you life and opportunity, whatever you saw would not continue to happen? Did you find yourself identifying what should be done that had not been done or not being done properly?

_____

_____

_____

5. What did that visit spark in your heart? Write them down as best as you can remember.

_____

_____

_____

6. Following that experience, did you find yourself wanting to know more about what it takes to deal with the situation, so you started searching for information? Do you intentionally visit some internet sites, read journals, watch movies, and even listen to discussions people are having on that issue?

_____

_____

_____

7. Since that time, have you been intentionally looking for opportunities to engage with issues surrounding that situation and its elimination from society?

_____

_____

_____

8. Do you occasionally see yourself in the center of those situations that got you angry and want to make a move to deal with it?

_____

_____

_____

9. Would you say that the program you are currently in is a result of the responses you gave to the questions asked above? If your answer is closer to yes than no, or far removed from can't really tell, you could be close to discovering your passion for life.

> **You have to understand that when something is your passion it hounds you and may give you sleepless nights, sometimes appearing in your dreams until you get up and want to do something about it, otherwise you only live in a world of fantasy.**

If someone says for example, "I hate it when people fall sick," or they say, "It hurts me each time some preventable death happened in a hospital or even in a house." The passion that goes with it is that you don't want to see people sick. You want to see them healthy all the time.

That is how career names like doctor, nurse, physician's assistant, pharmacist, radiologists, and the rest come up. The passion comes first and then you look for career opportunities to service that passion.

If you want to really know your purpose for life, it does not begin with your gift. What you may discover as your gift may be a link to several career names; so, the safest thing to start with is what makes you tick; what you strongly feel must be addressed in life.

There are people who use their gifts primarily to make money. That is scriptural: "Your gift will find a way before you and bring you before kings" (Pro 18:16).

Have you not read about a lot of people who are presented as celebrities, whose gifts have brought them great wealth and fame, and yet they end up frustrated in life? Some of them commit suicide.

When you operate your gift instead of following your passion, you can make some achievements in this life with some momentary rewards, and everyone sees you as great except that you may not be experiencing fulfillment in the real sense.

Passion goes beyond money. Money brings little satisfaction, but your passion will bring you satisfaction. There are people who use their money to pursue their passion. It means they first identified their passion.

What would you say, for example, about a footballer who after having made millions, he spends his money constructing and setting up hospitals in his home country? Would you say his purpose in life was playing football to entertain people or his purpose is to ensure that people with ailments are properly taken care of although he may not be a medical doctor?

Think through what I have shared and see if you can correctly identify your passion for life. If for all this while your passion has been misplaced, go back to God in prayer and talk with a matured Christian to help you find it back.

Here are samples of well-defined passions/purposes for living. Think of someone who has pledged and prayed to God that, for as long as God gives them life and health, they want to see the following situations and make these declarations:

For as long as God gives me life and good health...

1. There will be no injustice on earth. Men and women will be brought to the justice of God

and there will be equitable distribution of God's resources for all people irrespective of their ethnic background or their current circumstances. People will no longer live in fear of others who seek to create trouble wherever they go.

2. No man should fall sick on earth. I will do all in my power to ensure that people are equipped to live in health and wholeness; and that even if sickness attacks, they will receive the help needed to get sickness off their backs. People will no longer die prematurely of curable and preventable diseases in my world.

3. There will be no ignorance on earth. Men and women will know the truth about God and His creation, including what it takes to take advantage of God's green earth and enrich their lives on earth. I will give myself no rest until this is done with the help of almighty God.

4. I will raise a team to work together with me, and we will be totally committed to ensuring that there is no famine anywhere in the world, but that men will grow all they need to prevent hunger and always have food in abundance.

5. Happy homes will be the order of the day. People will be adequately prepared before they enter marriage and after that they will live happily together with the children God blesses to them. Families will come back as the first units established by God and they will fulfill God's plans and purposes for the family.

6. I am fed up with seeing people struggle to get a place to lay their head. Each time I walk in town in the evening and see people sleeping by the roadside something happens in my heart. My constant prayer to God is that all these will have a place to stay peacefully.

These are just a few samples of passion statements. If you find your passion there, identify it, write it, follow the pattern, and begin to pray fervently about it. Ask God to prepare you in every way to pursue and fulfill that with all the help available through the Holy Spirit.

_____

_____

_____

_____

Note that your passion is not to be a medical doctor, for example. You can see from these examples the passion that will drive someone to become a medical doctor. In the same way, you can see the passion that will drive someone to become a teacher or a pastor.

2.

DISCOVERING MY

SEED / NATURAL TALENTS

I want you to understand that the idea of gifts and talents or seed or whatever name men have given it did not originate from any man. It originated from God Himself. Gifts or talents come from the creative character of God.

They represent human manifestations of God's ability to bring things into being. God gave talents unto every man for the purpose of continued creativity.

God did not create houses and airplanes and bridges to cross. He did not create computers with all their accessories that help us communicate with our world. He put in us creative abilities to make these happen. Without those natural endowments from God, we could not have created anything.

We would still be living like the Stone Age. What we learned about the Stone Age is that they used stones to create fire. Even that comes from the creative capacity God endowed to men.

Since creation, God has used the creative ability He put in man to achieve a lot of purposes.

Read what God said when it came to creating the items for the temple and for the execution of ministry:

1 *Then the* L*ORD* *said to Moses,*

2 *"See, I have chosen Bezalel son of Uri, the son of Hur, of the tribe of Judah,*

3 *and I have filled him with the Spirit of God, with wisdom, with understanding, with knowledge and with all kinds of skills—*

4 *to make artistic designs for work in gold, silver and bronze,*

5 *to cut and set stones, to work in wood, and to engage in all kinds of crafts.*

⁶ Moreover, I have appointed Oholiab son of Ahisamak, of the tribe of Dan, to help him. Also I have given ability to all the skilled workers to make everything I have commanded you:

⁷ the tent of meeting, the ark of the covenant law with the atonement cover on it, and all the other furnishings of the tent—

⁸ the table and its articles, the pure gold lampstand and all its accessories, the altar of incense,

⁹ the altar of burnt offering and all its utensils, the basin with its stand—

¹⁰ and also the woven garments, both the sacred garments for Aaron the priest and the garments for his sons when they serve as priests,

¹¹ and the anointing oil and fragrant incense for the Holy Place. They are to

make them just as I commanded you."

Exodus 31:1-11

God called it the *spirit of wisdom and understanding* and also identified the several manifestations of the spirit: some for garments, some for woodwork, some for artistic designs, etc.

This means that if we are looking for someone's natural endowment, we are actually looking for what God deposited in him.

Over the years educationists and human development scholars have tried to catch a glimpse of the uniqueness of the individual. They used all manner of methods and instruments. Initially they called it intelligence and assigned numerical figures to it. For quite some time this method dominated the world of human development.

I am sure you are familiar with the term intelligent quotient or IQ. For several years this index was used to categorize people into who was more intelligent than others. If you took the test designed to test your intelligence and you scored high, you were deemed to be very intelligent, otherwise they tag you as not so intelligent.

Later, one man made a proposal which in some ways aligns with the biblical teaching on the spirit of wisdom and understanding in the Old Testament writings, as well as the gifts of the Spirit in the New Testament writings.

His writing taught that people are unique and should not be compared with others. Then he described the unique characteristics that people could possess and manifest differently. His name is Howard Gardner and he came out with endowments he called *Multiple Intelligences*. He called them multiple because there are several of them. He identified the following:

Visual-Spatial Intelligence

People who are strong in visual-spatial intelligence are good at putting/arranging objects in space to create beautiful scenes and scenarios. They are also able to paint and draw well. Think of them as people with a photo-memory of where objects are in the space. They find themselves and the ability to re-arrange things if they don't like what they see.

These individuals are often good with directions as well as maps, charts, videos, and pictures. They can look at designs and readily see patterns that others may not see.

These are the people that can come into your house and re-arrange furniture and everything in your sitting room and you stand amazed.

Does that describe you? Yes _____ No _____

Linguistic-Verbal Intelligence

People who are strong in linguistic-verbal intelligence are able to use words well, both when writing and speaking. They can easily remember information written or spoken. They enjoy reading and writing because they have a great vocabulary; words are not a problem to them. They are good at debating, have capacity to explain themselves well.

These individuals are typically very good at writing stories, memorizing information, and reading. Have you encountered someone who wants to sell a product to you and within a few minutes he has convinced you to buy something, and later you ask yourself, "What am I going to do with this?" in our part of the world you find them on the streets. People with verbal-linguistic intelligence have their way with words.

Does that describe you? *Yes* _____ *No* _____

Logical-Mathematical Intelligence

People who are strong in logical-mathematical intelligence are good at reasoning, recognizing patterns, and logically analyzing problems. These individuals tend to think conceptually about numbers, relationships, and patterns. They enjoy thinking in abstract terms, enjoy theorizing, finding reasons behind what they observe, enjoy thinking about complex situations and issues, enjoys engaging in analyzing situations, with the view to providing solutions to complex problems.

They don't enjoy routine thinking. Thinking that looks straight forward does not excite them. They want the complex ideas that demand multiple thinking patterns.

Does that describe you? *Yes* _____ *No* _____

Bodily-Kinesthetic Intelligence

Those who have high bodily-kinetic intelligence exhibit a high skill of moving their body and parts of their body in meaningful ways that provide great delight to onlookers. They perform meaningful actions with their body movements. They exhibit great hand-eye coordination. Mostly, they remember more by doing than hearing or seeing.

The obvious manifestation is that these are good at sports, dancing, and doing things with their hands. All the people you watch on TV in sports competitions possess body-kinesthetic intelligence.

Does that describe you? *Yes* _____ No _____

Musical Intelligence

People who have strong musical intelligence are good at thinking in patterns, rhythms, and sounds. They have a strong appreciation for music, can recognize musical patterns and tones easily, and exhibit tendencies to compose and perform music.

They enjoy singing and playing musical instruments. They are good at remembering songs and melodies, and they can understand musical rhythm and structure and notes.

Does that describe you? Yes _____   No _____

Interpersonal Intelligence

Those who have strong interpersonal intelligence have the capacity to assess accurately the emotions, intentions, desires and expectations of those around them. This perfect understanding of people usually makes them able to interact with the people around them with little struggle.

They are good at communication, both verbal and non-verbal levels, and easily create positive relationships with others. They have a great capacity to resolve conflicts between people and often get along with people quite easily.

Does that describe you? Yes _____ No _____

Intrapersonal Intelligence

Individuals who are strong in intrapersonal intelligence have the ability to assess and know themselves well; being aware of their own emotional states, feelings, and motivations. They engage in self-reflection and analysis, because it comes to them quite easily.

They are able to assess their strengths and limitations more accurately, and tend to always be on top of what is going on within themselves. They usually understand the basis for their own motivations and feelings, and are, therefore, described as having excellent self-awareness.

Does that describe you? Yes _____ No _____

Naturalistic Intelligence

Individuals who are high in this type of intelligence are more in tune with nature and are often interested in nurturing, exploring the environment, and learning about other species. These individuals are said to be highly aware of even subtle changes to their environments.

They show interest in subjects like botany [study of plants], zoology [study of animals] and tend to enjoy camping, gardening, and other outdoor activities that provide easy engagement with the natural world.

Does that describe you? Yes _____ No _____

The whole idea behind *Multiple Intelligences* is that it is inappropriate to expect the same level of performance from everyone in every endeavor of life. People should be allowed to manifest where they are naturally talented. Their performance in life should be measured in terms of what they are pre-wired to be able to do.

What we have to understand also is that though every human being is capable of manifesting all of these, people tend to be more endowed in a particular intelligence than with all others. That is what they would call their gift.

It is most unlikely that you find one individual who is endowed in equal strength in all eight identified intelligences. Occasionally, you may find someone who is good in two or at most three, but even in those instances, one of them stands out.

All the professions and career titles out there are closely linked and often tied to these. People endowed with verbal-linguistic intelligence for example are usually the ones who get involved in professions like journalism, media, law, teaching, authorship, and professions involving oratory expressions.

The above have been described as natural gifts to distinguish them from the gifts that become available to the individual when he becomes born again ad aligns his life with the Spirit of God. I will deal with spiritual gifts in another chapter.

I will end this chapter by saying that these natural endowments are equally coming from the Spirit of God. They come from the same source in that they represent God's creative ability in us.

The advantage that you have as a Christian is that when once you became a Christian, your natural endowments become enhanced and sharpened to achieve more than when you rely his natural strength.

Yes, the Holy Spirit can make you a better carpenter than you have been without Him. He can make you a better musician than without Him. He can make you a better engineer than without Him. It is the same God who works in us to do His work.

What you have to understand is that in the partnership with God to pursue your passion for life [which is your purpose for living], God uses both the natural endowments [talents] and the gifts of the Holy Spirit.

3.

DEVELOPING MY NATURAL TALENTS

It is appropriate for you to understand that both your natural endowments and the spiritual gifts are potential. They are like a seed. The normal thing you do to a seed is to sow it and let it grow. When it is fully grown into the tree that is originally locked inside it, then it can bear much more fruit than when it was a single seed.

If you have a single grain of corn and you eat it, the many grains that could have come out of it are all gone into your stomach. When you sow it, you get more corn from it, including more seeds to plant the next season.

Take the seed again. You plough your field, make sure it has enough water [moisture], air in the form of oxygen, nutrients and also ensure that the soil characteristics of your field are suitable to the growth of the seed; then you sow it. If these conditions are not properly met, your seed may sprout but cannot grow to its full potential.

Let me illustrate the importance of the environment for sowing by using the illustration that God made one day concerning the children of Israel, as recorded by Isaiah the Prophet of God:

1 *Let me sing for my beloved my love song concerning his vineyard: My beloved had a vineyard on a very fertile hill.*

2 *He dug it and cleared it of stones, and planted it with choice vines; he built a watchtower in the midst of it, and hewed out a wine vat in it; and he looked for it to yield grapes, but it yielded wild grapes.*

3 *And now, O inhabitants of Jerusalem and men of Judah, judge between me and my vineyard.*

4 *What more was there to do for my vineyard, that I have not done in it? When I looked for it to yield grapes, why did it yield wild grapes?*

⁵ *And now I will tell you what I will do to my vineyard. I will remove its hedge, and it shall be devoured; I will break down its wall, and it shall be trampled down.*

Isaiah 5:1-5

What is important here in this passage is not about the anger of the husbandman. What caused his anger was that he did everything he had to do to create the right environment for the seed to grow. It is only after it did not produce the expected fruit that the farmer got angry.

The point here is that if people do not plant their seed God has endowed them with in the right environment, making sure that it receives all the attention it needs, they have no business expecting good fruit from that seed. Now let's go for the real deal.

There are several situations in this world which constitute environments for different seeds to develop. It is left for the individual to find the most suitable environment. Let's look at some of them.

Family

Family, for example, provides the fundamental, in other words the first environment for the development of your natural endowment. Families are expected to help their children first to discover their gifts and also guide in its development into the form in which their gifts will become a blessing to themselves and their world at large.

Parents provide guidance for their children. They teach them values for life, show them a lot of love, live by example and do what God expects of them as parents.

It is more likely that parents prepare their children to be able to uphold their talents than actually develop the talent. Families where parents have fully developed their own talent are in a better position to help their children develop theirs as well.

If you come from a family where your parents have fully developed their God-given talent(s), you must do well to take advantage of that.

It does not mean your parents should tell you what to do. They are in position to help you in the process of developing your talent.

You have a role to play also. You are to submit to parental guidance, learn all you need to learn, including doing things that will enhance the development of your talent.

School

The next environment for seed development is school. Most people go to school for the wrong reasons – mainly because their parents want them to be in school. This is understandable because at a certain stage in your life you are not mentally ready to make the critical decisions for your life. Nevertheless, you have to grow beyond that.

To start with, you must see enrolment in school as an act that is critical to the development of your talent. That is what schools do. They develop whatever you have identified as your gift to the point your talents become functional skills in addressing issues around you.

Until your talent is developed into applicable skills, you are at best in a raw state of your creative potential.

Having enrolled in school for some years, you must move beyond seeing the school as your parents' idea. You must see the school as a credible, critical environment for you to grow your God-given talent.

The understanding that school is God's design and it is meant to help you grow your naturally endowed gifts goes a long way to help you go through school more meaningfully. The truth is that some students go through the school system, waste valuable time, let opportunities pass by, and they get out of school with little development of their creative potential. As a child of God, you must apply yourself to your studies and take advantage of the school resources to develop creativity.

The more you learn, the more food you are giving the seed in you to grow. The less you learn, the more you starve the seed in you, and it cannot grow to its full potential.

People who drop out of school, for example, refuse to take advantage of the opportunities the school provides for the development off their God-given talent. If you don't take school seriously and you graduate with a low performance or even fail to graduate, it is a reflection of how serious you took the environment provided for your development.

You don't have to wait until your final year in school before you start being serious. If you believed seriousness in your final year could bring you something good, how about starting level 100 with the same level of seriousness? You definitely would be better off with that.

Learning

You must understand that the primary reason you are in the secondary school or the university is to learn. That is the reason you parents pay fees and get you items that can help you learn, and make provisions that help you focus exclusively on your studies.

Learning is the single activity that directly affects the seed you are trying to grow as you prepare for your passion. Without learning your talent will continue in its raw form and will become of little use to you and your world.

Without learning, you could graduate from college and still feel unprepared to face life because your endowments from God are all dormant. They have not been activated because you did not commit yourself to learning. Let the development of knowledge and understanding be your number one goal.

You must discover your learning style and let that inform your engagement in classroom and in your private studies.

Take full advantage of all campus learning resources – lecturers, library, internet facility if you have them, as well as friends who you think can assist you develop yourself.

Be attentive and participate in class; see if you can capture as much during the class hour. Pace yourself to study material in bits instead of waiting until some exam.

Quickly adjust to campus life by following appropriate procedures and instructions; Put the early years behind you and be more responsible, more disciplined, make good friends, have a comprehensive timetable that covers both academic and non-academic activities to help you move along.

Personal Discipline

There is a lot of freedom as students enter university and other tertiary institutions of higher learning. All of a sudden, no one tells you when to sleep and when to wake up, etc. The challenge most students face is how to handle this freedom.

The watchword here is that freedom comes with a lot of responsibility. You become fully responsible for every action you take and for every activity you get involved in, including refusing to do what is expected of you.

Managing the freedom well guarantees overall good performance; otherwise you will waste all the years you spend at the university and your talent will remain underdeveloped.

Managing your time is very crucial to your personal development. Plan a timetable, do your best to follow it, and let your peers acknowledge your personal discipline when it comes to your time.

If you trade that to fit in to your friends' demands, you turn out the loser and you waste away your future. Unknown to you, some of those friends may be doing better than you in their academic studies, and you will realize this only after graduation.

Personal private studies and occasional group studies should help you feed your seed to grow and bring you into your expected end at graduation.

Top of the personal discipline is the development of morals. If you walk in Christian morals, you save yourself from a lot of trouble that come to students. As you study the Bible and fellowship with believers, let this translate to a commitment of moral and ethical behavior.

A lot of female students go through nightmares and sleepless nights due to emotional troubles inflicted by unhealthy relationships with undisciplined boys who are only interested in having sex with them. Do well to guard yourself against that.

When you violate exam regulation and get involved in malpractices, your future at the university hangs in the balance. Continual walking in this could lead to being expelled from school. That is also one sure way to graduate with high grades but unprepared for life.

Seek Counseling

Don't be shy to ask for all the help you need as you study in the university. Get help for academic, spiritual, moral and your career considerations. Help is available, but you have to seek it out. You are responsible for getting help you need. Don't be afraid to ask for help from your lecturers and academic advisors.

Counseling helps you adjust appropriately to university life. It helps you manage the influence of peers with self-defeating behaviors – alcohol, drugs, immoral behavior, rebellion towards authority, etc.

If your school has a chaplain, take the initiative to meet your chaplain and his team to freely discuss spiritual and moral issues confronting you in your life on campus. There is no shame about this. Every one of us at a point in time had needed a shoulder to cry upon, and those moments do not last forever if help is sought in good time.

If your school has a program to help you develop spiritually, make sure you participate in all activities organized by the school and other Christian groups on campus, and get the best out of these programs and activities.

4.

DEVELOPING YOUR SPIRITUAL GIFTS

The profile of uniqueness described above is common to all men wherever they are. When you become a Christian, God gives you the Holy Spirit as Jesus promised to all believers. That means you become a candidate of the gifts of the Spirit. The gifts of the Holy Spirit are given to individuals based on what God predominantly wants to use them to do in His kingdom.

4   Now there are varieties of gifts, but the same Spirit;

5   and there are varieties of service, but the same Lord;

6   and there are varieties of activities, but it is the same God who empowers them all in everyone.

7   To each is given the manifestation of the Spirit for the common good.

8   For to one is given through the Spirit the utterance of wisdom, and to

another the utterance of knowledge according to the same Spirit,

⁹ *to another faith by the same Spirit, to another gifts of healing by the one Spirit,*

¹⁰ *to another the working of miracles, to another prophecy, to another the ability to distinguish between spirits, to another various kinds of tongues, to another the interpretation of tongues.*

¹¹ *All these are empowered by one and the same Spirit, who apportions to each one individually as he wills.*

1 Corinthians 12:4-11

Each one must discover his or her spiritual gift and begin to exercise that gift. Like your natural endowments, don't let your spiritual gifts lie dormant.

Study what the apostle Paul wrote to Timothy, who was a young pastor of a church. You don't need to become a pastor for this exhortation to apply to you.

> [14] 'Do not neglect your gift, which was given you through prophecy when the body of elders laid their hands on you.
>
> [15] Be diligent in these matters; give yourself wholly to them, so that everyone may see your progress.'
>
> 1 Tim 4:14-15

The Apostle Paul exhorts that each man pay heed to the gift he has received from God. Stirring your gift means that you should not let the gift lie dormant. You have to put your gift to work. Don't let your spiritual gift remain underdeveloped.

Just as the development of your natural endowments is best enhanced in a school setting with formal instruction with examinations, etc., your spiritual gifts also need the right environment for them to develop. The most conducive environment for the development of your spiritual gift is the church.

By the church, I mean the body of Christ. Sunday services are not enough to enable anyone develop his spiritual gift. Sunday service, for example, is structured, with time constraints and often some rigid protocol that may not allow full expression of everyone's spiritual gift.

There are other avenues within the church world that the individual can take advantage of to develop their spiritual gift. Participate in Christian programs organized by the church, get involved in cell group activities where they exist, and simply look for avenues where you can exercise your spiritual gift.

Let me take you through a few of the spiritual gifts outlined in the passage.

The Gift of Discernment

This gift enables a person to know whether a statement made, or a behavior demonstrated is of God, human, or Satanic. It provides the ability to distinguish between truth and error, to know when a person or act is of God. Discernment also helps avoid heresies.

This is my spiritual gift:			
Yes		No	

The Gift of Knowledge

This gift helps the individual to uncover new insights, and understand the truths about God's word. He can easily discover, assemble, analyze and explain information related to the Christian faith and experience.

It gives the individual insight into how the word of God relates to a wide situations and circumstances people encounter in their Christian life. The truth about God comes to the individual as he encounters life's situations.

This is my spiritual gift:			
Yes		No	

The Gift of Wisdom

The gift of wisdom enables the individual to know the mind of the Holy Spirit and to receive insight into how knowledge may best be applied to specific needs arising in the Body of Christ. He is able to apply spiritual truth effectively to situations in your own life.

He extends this gift to guide others to intuitively arrive at a biblical solution to a problem facing them. They can choose the best from a number of possibilities to solve a problem. Where people are at a loss as to how to handle a problem, the individual with the gift of wisdom just makes a simple statement and the problem is on its way out.

This is my spiritual gift:			
Yes		No	

The Gift of Teaching

This refers to a special ability to communicate information, relevant to the health and ministry of the Body. It ends up edifying the hearers. The teacher conveys the truth of God to others with great clarity and brings both knowledge and understanding to those around.

Teachers are able to explain hidden truths of God's word that may not be obvious to all. Remember the Holy spirit is the author of the Scriptures. Whoever He gives the gift of teaching, therefore, is able to explain the mind of the spirit behind some of the passages of Scripture that are considered difficult to understand. In the process, they enable people to easily apply the word of God in their practical living.

This is my spiritual gift:			
Yes		No	

The Gift of Pastor

This gift enables the individual to take responsibility for the spiritual well-being of others. The person with this gift very often finds himself committed to offering spiritual oversight over a group of believers. The believer with this gift will have the confidence, capability, and compassion to provide spiritual leadership and direction for individuals or groups of individuals. They care for people's spiritual needs by teaching and guiding and helping them mature in Christ. They have the heart of a father. God, our heavenly Father, makes them real fathers with the heart to accommodate individuals in their congregation who are having a real hard time with life.

This is my spiritual gift:			
Yes		No	

The Gift of Evangelism

This gift empowers the individual to present the Gospel to unbelievers in a clear and meaningful way, which calls for a response. They are able to clearly articulate the story of Christ's death and His saving resurrection with simplicity, clarity, and effectiveness. The individual possessing this gift not only understands the Gospel, but feels a deep burden for those entrapped in the darkness of sin. They have a passion to get people saved and will hardly pass people without finding out if they have given their lives to Christ or not. They have a constant bubbling in their heart to share the gospel in season and out of season. Soul wining is their passion.

This is my spiritual gift:			
Yes		No	

The Gift of Exhortation

This gift enables the individual to stand beside fellow believers in need and bring comfort, counsel and encouragement so they feel helped. It is the ability to minister strengthening words of consolation to others such that they feel helped and healed. The gifted believer is able to reach out with Christian love and presence to people in personal conflict or facing a spiritual void. By virtue of this gift these people are motivated through encouraging words to live fruitful lives. Such individuals are usually sensitive to suffering, troubled and discouraged people and desire to help them.

This is my spiritual gift:			
Yes		No	

The Gift of Hospitality

This gift enables the Christian to open their homes [in fact, their lives] willingly and offer lodging, food, and fellowship cheerfully to other people. The Greek word for "hospitality" is philoxenia, meaning, "love of strangers."

This gift causes the believer to joyfully open his or her home for meetings and overnight visitors, making people feel welcomed and comfortable. Guests and strangers are graciously served.

The hospitable person is comfortable entertaining others - family, relatives, friends to be sure, but most especially when welcoming strangers. People with this gift have a special sensitivity with others, and they know how to make people feel at ease and wanted.

Making strangers feel comfortable and at home takes the form of a ministry that helps dispel loneliness and builds a sense of community.

This is my spiritual gift:			
Yes		No	

The Gift of Faith

This gift endows the believer with extraordinary confidence in God's promises, power, and presence. The individual is able to envision what God wants to happen and to be certain he is going to do it in response to prayer, even when there is no concrete evidence. There is discernment of the will and purpose of God for the future of his work. The believer with this gift is able to see the Spirit at work and trust the Spirit's leading without knowledge of the path ahead. The gift enables the individual to receive instant responses from God when they pray.

This is my spiritual gift:			
Yes		No	

The Gift of Mercy

The Christian with this gift feels exceptional empathy and compassion for those who are suffering. They are, thus, able to devote large amounts of time and energy to stand with them.

They are able to empathize with hurting people; they can feel their pain, and this leads them to do acts of service towards them. This ability to empathize with hurting people manifests itself into cheerful acts of service.

The believer feels deeply for those with physical, spiritual, or emotional needs and is motivated to take action to meet the needs. The actions taken reflect Christ's love.

Where they have financial resources, they make them available. Note that it does not take financial resources to have this gift. There are people with great wealth but do not have the gift of mercy.

This is my spiritual gift:			
Yes		No	

The Gift of Leadership

This gift enables the individual to easily mobilize and direct people towards attaining the goals set for the organization. Leaders have the extraordinary ability to get people to move along even if they don't feel like.

They tend to have a sense of vision and are futuristic in their orientation they look beyond the present and get people to do the same. They are always talking about what lies ahead and are not entrapped by the present circumstances. Leaders are usually visionary and that is what makes them ahead of many.

This is my spiritual gift:			
Yes		No	

The Gift of Administration

This is the ability to organize and guide human activity towards the execution of a program. The administrator has management ability and is able to direct and motivate people and coordinate activities.

They have the ability to organize and guide human activities in such a way that Christ's program is carried out; are able to devise and executes plans to accomplish goals of the church. They have special grace to manage, direct, and redistribute the resources of the church to designated activities and programs.

This is my spiritual gift:			
Yes		No	

The Gift of Service

This gift enables the individual to easily identify needs of the church that have not received the needed attention and use whatever resources God has given them to meet those needs.

The individual is empowered to willingly bear the burdens of other Christians so that they can do their tasks more effectively. They enjoy working behind the scenes to get God's work done.

They take burdens upon themselves and get things done. They place themselves at the disposal of others. Such individuals are always readily available when needed. This gift is sometimes described as the gift of helps.

This is my spiritual gift:			
Yes		No	

The Gift of Giving

This gift enables the individual to contribute their material resources to the work of the Lord liberally and cheerfully. This kind of giving from material blessings is characterized by exceptional willingness.

The believer is able to recognize God's blessings and to respond by generously and even sacrificially giving of one's material resources to support the Lord's work. Note that people with this gift may not necessarily have material goods in excess. Whatever little they have, they are enabled by the gift to share with others. Eventually, God blesses them with much material blessings to give more to more people.

This is my spiritual gift:			
Yes		No	

Growing your Spiritual Gift

Whatever spiritual gift you have, it will bless a lot of people if it us nurtured to mature. You need to grow this gift because the situations where this gift may be required vary from place to place and from circumstance to another.

If you have the gift of giving, for example, you know that the need to give toward the construction of a library for the youth department may be greater than the need to give toward a youth program in a village nearby.

The same is applicable to all the gifts. People with word of knowledge, for example, must grow in the exercise of the gift so they can exercise the gift in the most appropriate ways.

You must mature in exercising your spiritual gift because when your spiritual gift operates like an amateur and not a professional, you become less effective in the exercise of the gift.

Go Back to the Word of God

There is one sure way to grow the gift. Go back to the word of God. The Bible has several instructions concerning how to use the gift you have from God. If you don't know these Scriptures and how they relate to the exercise of the gift, you have the gift alright, but you may not be as effective in its exercise as you could be.

Take the gift of discernment, for example. Study what the Bible has to say about discerning good from evil. Use Bible study aids like commentaries.

1. The following verses deal with discernment and false teachings: Eph. 6:12; 2 Cor. 11:13-15; 2 Pet. 2:1-3; 1 John 4:1-3; 1 John 4:6;Matt 16: 21-23; Acts 5:1-11; Acts 8:20-23; Acts 13:6-12; Acts 16:16-18; Rev. 2:2; Rev. 2:14-15,20.

Do a study of the Bible for all other gifts, especially what you discover as your gift.

Develop your Human Spirit

Your spirit is described in the book of Job as the candle of the Lord. Paul in the letter to the church in Rome wrote that the Spirit bears witness with our spirit that we are the children of God. The truth in these verses is that God communicates to you through your spirit. That is why it is important to develop your spirit.

When you develop your spirit, it becomes sharper and more sensitive to the Holy Spirit. That is when you can receive all God wants to teach you. When your spirit grows, it makes the exercise of your spiritual gifts easier as well.

You sharpen your human spirit if you pray often in tongues. Pray with your understanding as often as you can, but pray with your spirit so as to make your spirit grow.

Practice listening to your human spirit by being still before God. Sometimes we are too noisy to allow our spirit to be quiet before God.

5.

TAKING MY GENERATION

BY MY ANOINTING

18 *"The Spirit of the Lord is on me, because he has anointed me to proclaim good news to the poor. He has sent me to proclaim freedom for the prisoners and recovery of sight for the blind, to set the oppressed free,*

19 *to proclaim the year of the Lord's favor*

Luke 4:18-19

This is the powerful statement Jesus made at the very early stage of His ministry on earth. It is a loaded statement of purpose, passion and enablement. In this passage Jesus makes it clear why He came. He had no doubts regarding why He was on earth in human form and how He had been equipped to carry out His ministry.

The declaration also shows God's pattern in equipping individuals to carry out His purposes on earth. He anoints them with His Spirit and with power. You have to start seeing yourself as one of such individuals God is seeking to partner with on earth for kingdom agenda on earth. It means you have to see yourself as equipped to stand in partnership with God on earth.

Have you identified your passion from reading what I have discussed earlier on? Have you identified your natural abilities? What about your spiritual gifts? If you have been able to identify all this within yourself, then you are anointed to take your generation. That is all you need.

All you need to take your world for God and our Lord Jesus Christ is the full development of your natural talent and your spiritual gift(s) and operate under the anointing of the Holy Spirit.

You don't need to grow up into a man or woman before you start taking territories for the kingdom of God. You can start wherever you are now, even as a young growing person. If you think deeply, you will realize that you have what it takes to win your peers for Christ and help them go through their teenage and young adult years with the anointing God has endowed you with.

Winning your Peers for Christ

There are a lot of young people living today who have not yet given their lives to Christ. As a young person yourself, you probably are privy to what might be keeping them outside the kingdom of God. It means then, that you are in position to offer yourself as an available vessel unto God.

You understand their vocabulary, you speak their language, you can interpret their mannerisms, and they can more easily identify with you that they would with an adult. Most young people think anything that comes from an adult is out of touch.

They hear with their ears, but it may not easily spark a response from them like it would if they hear those same things from a young person using all that defines young people today.

I trust you are getting the picture. You have the natural endowments which attract youth; you have discovered your spiritual gift; and you understand your peers; so, you are good to go!

Start by targeting those in your immediate environment, like your dorm or hostel, whichever is applicable. The best approach is to isolate people from the crowd and deal with them on a one-on-one basis. That way they are more sober and they listen more attentively.

All kinds of things happen if you try to witness to people in a group. It makes people hide behind the real issues. In private, they may even be able to open up to you and tell you the struggles they are going through in their life.

Challenging them by your Creativity

At this point in your life, you have not started you career, but you have your academics. A good display of knowledge and understanding of the subjects taught in class, for example, sets you apart and makes you the attention of your peers. That is your creativity at work at this stage of your life. When your peers discover that you exhibit brilliance in your academics, they naturally get drawn to you.

They want you to explain topics and concepts that they find difficult to understand. They want to be in your study group because they see you as an academic expert. They want to be associated with you because you come out as an "A" student.

As long as someone wants to do well in their academics as you do, you are already influencing them. This may not immediately result in the conversion of some of them to Christ, but it definitely creates healthy forum when you can eventually share the gospel with them. If you are already sharing the gospel with them, helping them in their academic work becomes an added motivation.

Influencing by your Special Talent

Apart from the display of excellence in your academic work, your natural gift or spiritual gift also is a potential avenue or influence. Granting that you have the gift of music for example; you become a point of rallying because a lot of young people love music and music tends to be a powerful crowd puller among young people.

Don't sing only in your bathroom. Sing in church, sing also to your friends in very informal settings, share what you are learning in the world of music with them and let them generally enjoy this gift you have.

Your generation is the cyber generation. The more you show yourself as a guru in information technology and related issues, even if you are not enrolled in an IT program, your knowledge and deep understanding of IT pulls your friends around you.

Leading by Christian Character

When as a young Christian your life is above reproach, you become a magnet that draws people your age. They get challenged by your morals and commitment to ethical standards. You can be sure that even some of the people who call you names because you are always talking about Christ and see Christian principles manifested in your life are secret admirers.

They may not have come to you like Nicodemus came to Jesus, but they want you to be who you are because it gives them hope that one day things will be well with them too.

Get ready to take your world.

CHECKLIST

Now that you have prayerfully read this booklet, seeking God's face as you read along, check those you are now able to do:

☐ Identify what lies deep within your heart that you want to live to pursue as your passion and purpose for life

_____

_____

_____

_____

☐ Know what endowments God has placed within you, both your natural gift as well as the spiritual gifts

_____

_____

_____

_____

☐   Know and understand what to do to develop your natural gift(s)

_____

_____

_____

_____

☐   Know and understand what to do to develop your spiritual gift(s)

_____

_____

_____

☐ Start doing things towards influencing your generation

---

www.ingramcontent.com/pod-product-compliance
Lightning Source LLC
Chambersburg PA
CBHW061754020426
42331CB00006B/1474